MUSEUM OF DREAMS

Poetry by
Roger Granet

To Lena-

Your future is
only filled with
goodness + growth.
with sincerity

Rg 5/98

ROSS-HUNT PUBLISHING, P. O. Box 28, Thornwood, NY 10594

MUSEUM OF DREAMS
by Roger Granet

Edited by Linda Raskin

Cover design and illustrations by F. Elliot Siemon

Library of Congress Catalog Card Number 97-92785

Printed in the United States of America

FIRST EDITION
1997

ISBN # 0-9659661-3-5

ACKNOWLEDGMENTS

The author would like to thank the following publishers for permission to reprint material copyrighted by them:

The New York Times "Metropolitan Diary" for:

"Action/Camera*"*
"Between the Seasons*"*
"Brooklyn Baseball"
"Christmas Wrappings"
"Cycles"
"Dads/Daughters"
"December (on Christmas Eve)"
"Dreams"
"Fathers"
"Father's Day"
"February 14th"
"Fourth of July"
"Halloween"
"Indian Summer"
"January at Fifth Avenue"
"July Fourth"
"Love's Lease"
"May"

"Montauk at Dusk"
"New Year"
"New Year's Morning"
"New Year's (Now and Then)"
"Nuts"
"School Days"
"Seasonal Sentences"
"Street Fair"
"Summer Rental"
"Summer Vacations"
"Thanksgiving"
"Thanksgiving Eve"
"Thanksgiving Parades"
"The Chef"
"The Fourth"
"True Romantics"
"Valentine's Day"
"Verbal Valentines"

Cornell University Medical College Alumni Quarterly for:
"Appointments" "Persona" "Sessions"

Outlook for:
"Foul"

Beachcomber for:
"Summer Moments"

Night Roses for:

"Generations" "Marketplace"

CONTENTS

DEDICATION

To the women who own my heart:
Valerie, Courtney and Jamie
and
To the friends and family
who lease it from them.

I

DREAMS

NEW YEAR'S MORNING

A newborn new year
arrives earlier than expected
and joins me at the breakfast table
through the white steam of black coffee.

Hungry to know,
starving to predict,
this newfound new day
feasts on fantasies, tastes tomorrow.

And hoping to get
a head start on possibilities
the future suddenly becomes now.
All of this, all at once, this morning.

DREAMS

Someone
should walk the streets
collecting dreams
since those of us
who work at sleep
seem too tired to do the job.

Somewhere
the task of saving memories must
be recorded. Perhaps a storehouse
might hold them in golden barrels.

Sometimes
in the morning, sturdy souls
forget the nighttime fragments of
black and white recollections
that weave in and out of sunlight
like elusive flashy photographs.

There has to be
a permanent collection,
a museum of dreams.
Somehow.

NUTS

Squirrels, it seems, lead lovely lives.
On Sunday mornings they probably
play hide and seek between wild
flowers instead of sneaking cigarettes or
pushing power mowers over jungled lawns.

Squirrels, most certainly, have hearts
and hopes and tree trunk homes
but if they could, they probably would
laugh out loud at mortgage payments and
flat out scoff at overdrawn bank accounts.

Squirrels, no doubt, would ignore
early hour alarm clocks and late night
messages on fancy phone machines. Instead,
acorns and Spring rains reinforce their dreams.
One would be nuts not to be a squirrel.

VALENTINE'S DAY

When I was twelve
I bought hazel-eyed Holly
a doily covered box of candy
that would clearly win her heart.

Alas, instead she plucked at
the lacy bow with only ennui
and annoyance and snapped
my hopeful sixth grade soul.

Defeated and denied I got
high on Nehi and penny pretzel rods
and gave up girls (until the next week)
and forgot Valentine's Day (until the next year).

But last month at our high school reunion
Holly asked me to dance and holding her
in a distant dip of memories I recalled the
bittersweetness of being twelve and in love.

JULY FOURTH

I have this memory,
perhaps a dream
of when some hip savvy sisters
took their kid brother
to a funky July Fourth parade.

Nourished by cotton candy and love,
dazzled by sparklers and sunsets
he stares up at Uncle Sam on stilts
and is blinded by full firecrackered skies.

And his sisters hold his sticky hands
and kiss his five-year-old happy heart
until he is safely, softly tucked
into another sweet, safe night,
in this dream, perhaps this memory.

BROOKLYN BASEBALL

As a kid, me and my best friend
Jerry caught a Night Game at
Ebbets Field and watched the Dodgers
beat the Giants just before Da Bums
abandoned us and beat it out of Town.

Podres was unstoppable, a smooth
Southpaw with a slippery slider.
And Junior Gilliam ate up every
grounder at Second with the graceful
gait of a gifted ballet dancer.

Peanuts and Pop-ups held our hearts.
And in the Ninth, Campanella hit
a homer so high that I knew New York
owned every star in the sky and that
baseball belonged in Brooklyn forever.

SUMMER RAIN

Unremarkable
and unobtrusive
these tired aimless hours stretch
past the burned out yellowed morning and
nap through the played out amber afternoon

Until all at once
with the swift élan
of nature's sleight of hand
night falls
as does a steady Summer rain.

SUMMER VACATIONS

On Summer vacations
while driving endless hours
down laugh lined highways

We tell our kids the same story
they have heard a million miles before:
"We met outside Shea Stadium at a

Beatles' concert back in high school."
And they always roar with mirth (the
notion of our youth is incredulous to them).

They can't believe that John, Paul,
George or Ringo could possibly be our age
since on MTV, the Fab Four are ageless.

And on Summer vacations, we smile
at ourselves (what parental fools we
be who try to prove a point to teens)

Until we stop to sleep after a Hard
Day's Night and Imagine Yesterday
and suddenly I Want to Hold Your Hand...

MONTAUK AT DUSK

With wine and lobsters and
love

We watch the wide Moon
kiss

The slight Sun goodbye
behind

A dancing purple bay
filled

With yachts and turtles and a
wet

Briny mirror of us reflected as
one.

AUGUST

Dusk, tired and dreamy
yawned past the
yellow day.

And now, this silent evening sleeps,
a lazy Summer remnant
of an easy errant August,

A Season acting out
against the rules
against the dawn.

NÉE AUTUMN

Summer swelled
towards term
distended
and sluggish

Then all at once
she contracted
effaced
and dilated

Announcing
with pastel hues
and soft
silent breezes

Fall's
natural
spontaneous
delivery.

INDIAN SUMMER

Beneath a fat down quilt
and this September rain
I lie in bed with

wide-eyed consciousness
projecting Rorschach remnants of August
onto the Summer's ceiling:

of long lazy weekends
wrapped in slow quiet breezes
and frothy high-topped waves.

And ignoring this night's
movement towards
a pale cool dawn

I disclaim the reality
of Summer nearly lost
and Fall barely found.

HALLOWEEN NIGHT

Tonight, well past work and classrooms
anyone can be anybody
as we climb inside our costumes.

Down the Village
grown-ups ignore phone bills while
in the Suburbs
children forget about homework.

At these black and orange hours
we can make believe beneath a Fall moon
and pretend against an Autumn breeze.

And throughout the playful evening
full faced pumpkins only smile at fantasy
as ghosts and goblins scare off
reality until deep into tomorrow.

AUTUMN

These busy boundless hours
are waxed with work
waned of play.

Suddenly there seems to be no time
to pause, to love, to watch
the start of auburn afternoons.

Fall, too fast
too full, the Autumn
of these amber days.

THE MARKETPLACE

My wife suggested
it was our misfortune that
the effort I invested in writing poetry
did not pay off in lots of DOLLARS or dividends.

"Perhaps," she mused (we have different
muses, although I love her deep into the future
and forever), "if you shunted your focus
to the stock market, we might be rich!"

I wondered:
"Is there no wealth in poetry?"
Alas, verses are not traded on the Big Board
like pork belly futures or copper calls.

But what if Wordsworth sold at
Twenty two or Keats at Fifty four?
I wonder if Dickinson would split two for one.
A STOCK EXCHANGE OF POETRY?
Imagine such an imagining.

THANKSGIVING

Everyone wants to go home
for Thanksgiving

Wherever home is.

Not just you and me
but the uptown fancy folks and
the downtown down-and-outers

Whoever they might have been.

Way back then, we were laughing
wide-eyed children at tables
heavy with turkey and dressing and pies

Whenever that once was.

And now savoring tastes of long gone
times, we re-collect sweet birds of youth

whatever that must have been.

SPORT

On my college baseball team
I only wanted to be the catcher
in the rye, but Coach never understood
my constant request and sent me back
out to third base to block doubles up the line.

He would tilt his grey
haired head at me and wonder out loud
"Hey, kid, what's a catcher do in the rye?"

And when the Season ended
I played with his children at the
park on weekends and helped them
giggle on the seesaw and kissed their tears
from freeze-tag falls

Until Coach relented with a glare then a glint
and said "O.K., next year you can do whatever a
ballplayer does as the catcher in the rye."

DECEMBER
(ON CHRISTMAS EVE)

Our Living Room, swollen
stuffed and out of control, is

nothing like the dreamy scenes of the
Christmas cards toppled on the mantel.

Only The Tree seems in order —
standing at attention, proud and steady

like an overdecorated Army Officer.
Yet somehow, the gifts will get wrapped

and the stockings will be hung as we
beat the deadline of this December dawn,

breathless, spent and hopeful that we
might survive beyond next week's New Year.

II

PARTNERS

GENERATIONS

Time becomes gossamer twine
in arthritic hands of older men.

My father told me that when
I was too young to know its meaning.

No, he never did tell me
but I wish he had before he died.

The gossamer twine is mine now
but that ownership confers no power.

My children might have children soon.
What will I tell them of this lease called life?

Maybe something sage to hold onto
since generations seem deaf to connections.

Too mute is love between parents and
progeny while time becomes gossamer twine.

And hope calls out quietly for
memories as a chance to hear our futures.

NEW YEAR'S (Now and Then)

Tonight
clothed in black tie and propriety
we squint back at yesterdays' New Year's
Celebrations
when we dressed in bell bottoms and defiance
and railing against the formality of this

Evening
we sneak off in gentle rebellion
as we kiss the year goodnight and
Whisper
of our love born in peace and
protest into the morning.

PARTNERS IN TIME

I saw you for a moment
this morning
somewhere after the alarm clock
and sometime before our
groggy-eyed kids awoke and

I saw you for a second
this evening
between an endless infinity of
homework and
stretched out bedtime stories, but

I see you now as we wind our way
to bed
forgetting our fatigue and
remembering each other
as we close the day
and unlock our night.

NEW YEAR'S DAWN

The early easy Sun
shuffles across the new found new year

as last night's celebrations
disappear like wind washed confetti.

And while a quiet unmarked morning
highlights silent sober hours

the cold clear dawn squints at sleepy
possibilities and awaits awakening potentials.

VERBAL VALENTINES

We whisper
"We" a lot

our hearts punctuated
by plural pronouns

and as night
runs on into morning

so do our sentences
as we hold each other

in period, paragraph
and exclamation point!

TRUE ROMANTICS

On the night before Valentine's Day
before all the

fancy chocolates and all the overpriced roses
true romantics snuggle up

to the commonplace, cuddle up with the mundane.
Somewhere among the

clutter of toys and the cacophony of teenagers
long married couples

search everywhere for playful carefree cupids.
And holding hands

they kiss and hug on well worn couches knowing
that the reality

of love is the warm width of intimacy over
lots of time.

WE

Together
tonight
and into the morning

I seldom thought of
thinking of other women
as we held reality and each other

although
tonight
I thought of you
when we were younger

and into the morning
I looked at you
and wondered of us
when we will be older

together
tonight
and into the morning.

IMAGES

I know him,
now
after hidden years of
"Father Knows Best" imaginations
when he was more a character than
a person

and I would
see him as one long T.V. Series
without commercials
or Summer reruns,

until I
cancelled him
on the screen and he became
alive, flawed
and loved
at last and

real.

WEDNESDAY MORNING LOVE

Black hair
long full straight
almost perfect on a
Saturday night when blush
hides freckles and mascara
masks an overworked mom.

But I
love her
more on Wednesday
morning with oily
hair freckled face
tired eyes and children.

MARCH

At this time of year
the hours seek no holidays
the minutes demand no celebration
as sleepy moments yawn
at quiet calendars.

Perhaps the ambling weeks
search for expectations
that feel reasonable
seem reachable yet still
stretch our hopeful hearts.

So embracing cold
clear days, all we need
is the warmth of our
relationships, since love
strong, like a March wind, is now.

HOMELESS

A long time ago
she would have been someone else
from somewhere else

and perhaps she used to laugh
at "Leave it to Beaver" and
play kick the can and

even ate grape jelly sandwiches
with her grandfather
before her life was

wrapped in layers of
discarded clothes and detached memories of
a long time ago.

ALWAYS LOVE

Tangled
like the roots of ageless trees
deep in the woods of New Hampshire
we grew together
and became old as grandparents

And the Sun warmed us
at times burned us
as the sheltering limbs
struggled to offer protection
against rain snow

tears
joy sadness
sorrow glee
pain and
always love.

SEASONAL SENTENCES

Days of May suggest
grand greeting cards.

If Weather were
a literary lion
words would fall
from typewriters like
petals windblown from
flowered fields.
A Hallmark Hall
of Fame, this

Bright bold month
written in boundless blossoms.

EXISTENTIAL WEDNESDAYS

If we choose to face up
to it on a Wednesday morning
life is really about abandonments
disconnections and loves lost.

But who wants to deal with
such angst at early hours
with coffee and The Times when
if truth be told we would rather read
about fancy foods and movie listings.

Yet between you and me and
this random convoluted world of ours
life, at least, is really the converse too:
the potent attachments and robust
connections and thankfully, hopefully great
big loves just about found.

THE FOURTH

Unannounced
the sky erupts
with a cacophony of colors
as we gulp the night,
a Family fused in hugs and giggles
beneath scintillating scotomas
of hues and booms.

Until a lightless silence
sends us
softly shuffling home
with hands held tight
to sleep in red, white and
blue dreams of growing up and
old together.

LOVE POEM

One night way back
in the sixties between anti-war
protests and pre-med studies
I wrestled with the maudlin words
of a sleepy college student.

Deep into untouched hours
I tossed and turned
stilted verses of loving you
forever and holding you
whenever it became too cold or dark.

And now, decades later
with children older than we were
when we met, I am still maudlin
still loving you and still holding you
whenever it becomes too cold or dark.

DOORMAN

Uniformed in pride and vigilance,
a mobile guard from Buckingham,
he patrols the concrete as he has for 30 years.

A commander of "All deliveries to the rear,"
A catcher to future Hall of Famers,
A coddler of endless hungry newborns.

But recently on the subway to his walkup,
he is sad; for as Winter overshadows Fall he
knows the laws of apartments (and Nature).

And most nights, sitting in silence,
he polishes his silver whistle with dawn
dreams of halting wild taxis for one more Season.

SUMMER TIME

Like clockwork, each and every Summer
we fall in love again
Again.

Somehow the hot hearty Sun and the
cool carefree waves tick off
Romance.

And as August hugs July so do we
as our happy hearts rewind, unalarmed
Anew.

SUMMER RENTAL

On August nights, sleep seeks
no boarders, finds no tenants
while lovers deny darkness.

When it becomes late enough
each of us has
the right to own bright skies as

Ray after ray of sweet-talk
falls across ceiling shadows
illuminating tenderness.

Everywhere, couples held in sudden
sunshine, squint past quiet clocks,
stare at hands held close to joy.

And Summer only rents to hopeful hearts
since love sees no blackness
only the light of August nights.

LOVE

tonight
i dreamed
of holding her
forever, forever,
relentless photographs
inside my sleeping
over active head

until it
hurt so much
that my rem broke wide open
and so did we

when i woke her up
in vivo
to play out for real
the dream
of holding her
forever, forever
tonight.

KIOSK MAN

Framed by a patchwork
of newspapers and magazines
the kiosk man sits inside
his plywood hut and
sawed off gloves

and somewhere
in between
the yawning Sun and
the late night buses
we rush past him

as if he were an
automated teller machine
and never wonder where
he sleeps or when he plays
or whom he loves.

STREET FAIR

The bright, but
tired afternoon Sun
refracts through
prisms of people

and fans out
towards a rainbow of
home made jewelry, dog eared paperbacks,
and blocks of forever food

until tugged gently
into the unfolding night
by overblown balloons and
sleepwalking children.

FALL

Preoccupied and neglectful of the
Seasons, we never seem to notice
Change.

As morning's breeze calls
Autumn
And Central Park shouts
October

We remain ignorant and unaware
until day demands night and
we finally fully listen to
the cool clear cries of
Fall.

CHRISTMAS WRAPPINGS

Today my kids
sit on the Store Santa's lap
wrapped in bright dreamy promises

as I watch
boxed inside my own
distant December memories

forgetting for now
overcredited credit cards and
the rude reality of tomorrow's big bills.

III

FATHERS

FATHERS

My grandfather (who I
called Popsy)
was a Bricklayer from Bayonne and
wore spats and smoked stogies
and at five foot four
could expand any room with grins
and goodness.

And my father (who I
called Pops)
was a CPA in Suburbia and
wore pleated pants and smoked Camels
and at five foot nine
could stretch any house with smiles
and sincerity.

And my kids' father (who they
call Pop)
is a Shrink in the City and
wears well worn memories and chews gum
and at six foot one
hopes for the same wide warmth that Pops
and Popsy had to fill his family's hearts.

DADS/DAUGHTERS

Somehow, in a wink of time
Junior became Senior.
That cherubic, clingy kid who
wore mischief for makeup

And used laughter as lipstick has
forgotten all about Oscar and Big Bird,
rejected playdates with Ken and Barbie.
Instead, dressed in dreamy adolescence

She wears the future with poise and
presence. And while I am sizing up
her prom partner and gearing up for her
high school graduation, I reluctantly

Release this lovely lady, somehow reassured
that in another blink of years
Junior might become a mother, which
would make me, gulp, gasp, a grand-dad!

MATERNAL LAUREATES

At these wild waking hours
dads and daughters danced in
last night's dreams, wander
randomly through their houses
breaking every Law of Physics.

Without vector or direction
these helpless, hapless souls
make weak attempts at perking
strong coffee and empty efforts
at clearing up endless clutter.

And finally accepting failure
and futility, they wonder with
hungry hearty love if it's time
to stir the noble Nobel winning
women still deep in sleep upstairs.

MAY

Dawn
paints shadows
tiger-striping taxis.

Haze
moves morning
air-brushing frowns.

Warmth
stains midday
sun-burning lovers

As
this May month
yawns in yellows.

FATHER'S DAY

Like some stubble-faced King
in his suburban court, I will
rule this sunny Sunday with
the pretense of paternal power.

And my progeny, like royal subjects,
will pretend that I am the regal ruler!
Sermons from the college freshman on
yuppie greed and greenhouse effects
will surcease and her high school sister
will abandon earringed boyfriends
and loud late-night music.

All until tomorrow when I will surrender
my crooked crown and, dethroned but
still loved, accept the reality that daughters,
not dads, possess the family royal ancestry.

CHAMP

The kid struts
home from soccer practice
spitting on innocent lawns.

Tall, sweaty, bruised
and gruff
groaning into the shower.

Then locker room talk
at the dinner table with
a strong victory voice.

Meat and potatoes
chased by Gatorade
then off to do pushups.

And only twelve years old:
what a terrific little
lady.

FOURTH OF JULY

One July Fourth
my wife and kids and I sat
and struggled to write a poem in tribute —

alas, it was an endless empty effort
to fill rigidly rhymed verse with trite
hot dogs, stilted firecrackers and clichéd skies

until with grins and shrugs we quit
and turned to the TV, a family penned
together and warmly watched a screen explode

in unrhymed

love

and free verse

celebration.

THE CHEF

I bought a brand new over-priced
barbecue grill
with an automatic starter and
permanent coals and
no matter how hard I try the
cheeseburgers will never be rare and

The corn never sweet but my kids
will say, "Don't worry, Dad,"
and I won't because you
don't eat
hugs and giggles and kisses
anyway.

FEARS AND FATHERS

Can I convince you
that all of those monsters
beneath your bed are nothing more
than the potent power of your
imagination?

Will you believe me
when I tell you that the dangerous
dinosaurs outside your window are
only the endless expanse of your
fantasies?

Will I win my point
that the wild wilderness
of our backyard is merely the
boundless bounty of your
creativity?

We both might get some sleep
if you understood that the night
is simply day without light
darkened by the depth of
love.

JOGGING
(Along Route 102 in Lee, Massachusetts)

Flying grasshoppers
(but I was certain they were extinct)

Purple wildflowers
familied with clusters of crabgrass

Bus breezes against
an overheated Summer wind

Green, green leaves
behind sleeping ski lifts

Rocks, forever in formation
creased with limestone cheshire smiles

Butterflies, the color of halloween
in playful flight to nowhere

And constant Speed Limit signs
(but who would want to speed)?

AUGUST'S END

Dreamy days
Lie still and sleepy
Beneath a full-faced moon.

Suntanned nights
Sit mute and weary
Deaf to August's imminent end.

Only sleep stirs
With newborn noises as
The morning yawns in quiet colors.

And the final sounds of Summer
Speak in hushed memories and
Whispered recollections.

SCHOOL DAYS

Like proud soldiers
on the way to a foreign land
kids go off to kindergarten:
straight backed four foot warriors
with any separation anxiety
hidden deep within their backpacks.

Yet wounded worried
parents are in disarray, wrecked
by this abandonment, devoid of
stoicism as tears and sniffles
forever damage designer
suits and ties.

But somehow both
Moms and Dads will survive, buoyed
by endless papier-maché pumpkins,
tons of crayola drawn pilgrims and
finally surplus superglued Santas when
Christmas vacation, at last, arrives.

BUGGED

When I was a kid
I used to count the dots

On ladybugs' backs, always searching
for six, since my science teacher said
that one was the queen.
But now that I am older,
almost old, as my kids might say,
I realize that there is no queen

And that makes me sigh and
so does being older.

SUBURBAN MORNINGS

Dogs bark
back and forth from fenced
in yards like adolescents
chatting late at night and

Moms carpool
kids in well washed wagons
with the fierceness and finesse
of cops on high speed chases while

Suited dads
yawn at take out coffee
cups and skim the local paper
at well worn train stations as

Suburban mornings
stretch out with the sweet
symmetry of freshly cut lawns and
the flowered rhythm of newborn dawns.

AUTUMN AWAKENINGS

On the cusp of consciousness
near the edge of wakefulness
we all behave like children
not unlike our own children.

Grumpy and angry with the dawn
cranky and annoyed at the morning
we demand one last chance to dream
expect one more turn at sleep.

And as time Falls along
with newly windblown leaves
we grudgingly greet the reality of
adulthood and this early amber Autumn day.

MATURATION

After all these years
we still get scared when
it thunders late at night

and cry in front of crowds
at funerals of old friends

and laugh at sitcom reruns
with our growing children
and love to do the Lindy at weddings

with grey in our hair
after all these years.

HALLOWEEN

Dusk
calls out to candied kids who
bellow back in raucous fright and

Evening
screams past pumpkins, goblins and
wind wild leaves while

Night
shouts in chilled laughter and
ignores unfinished homework as

Tomorrow
winks at the expansive delight and
sleeps softly in gentle celebration.

THANKSGIVING EVE

Sitting

on the tired tailgate
of a station wagon at a
rest stop on the thruway
I stare through the steam
of a light, no sugar coffee

Watching

three lanes of a highway lined with
all night truckers in overdrive
restless relatives in Greyhounds
new college students in old used cars and

Squinting

past well worn toll booths
I smell starving smiles and
taste the hungry reconnections
that will fill all the
families down the road tomorrow.

FALL FLIGHT

Supine and
staring through the
matrix of maple limbs
and chlorophyll laced leaves

I am
an air traffic controller
guided by the puffing patterns
of Autumn winds and

the late
narrow Sun, as I announce
the imminent arrival of
sticky helicopter seedlings

somewhere in
transit between the full
Fall afternoon and the runway
of this sleepy suburban lawn.

SONS' FATHERS

I love my father and
I miss my father.

When youth knew no safety
he held my hand against thunder,
he soothed my soul as savvy girls
broke my naive heart.

What are these stilted words
between sons and dads?
Why can't we speak about the
sweet strength of our connections?

I still love my father and
I still miss my father.

IV

CYCLES

NEW YEAR'S DAY

As we start again, Again
At the nidus of the new year
On this newborn tableaux rosa,
Why must we always re-invent ourselves?

Can't we see through last
Night's celebrations when we pretended
To pretend and only viewed a
Valid opacity, an obscure truth?

Yet this morning it must
Be clear that who we are within
The Seasons seeks no apologies,
Searches out no forgiveness

For Nature knows all of
Our goodness, a golden vision
Of sutured psyches refracted through the
Prisms of harmless sins and gentle lies.

NEW YEAR'S RESOLUTIONS

It's time once more
to dust off all those
"No Mores" and
"Never Agains"

and to polish the
"Promises" and
"Cross My Hearts"
because

they haven't
been used at all
since
last year.

JANUARY AT 5TH AVENUE

Underneath the
Don't Walk...Don't Walk sign
strangers like snowflakes
collect at City corners and

push into anonymous drifts
against the wind
against the night

until they pull apart
plowed by the
Walk...Walk message

and the chill
and the Winter.

SLEET

Unwilling or unable to
commit to rain or snow, sleet suggests
an ambivalence only Winter knows.

Warm skewed views frame
a deceptive tame translucence from
urban apartments and country kitchens.

Yet sleet, like a cold heart, immobilizes.
Nature, make up your mind: Love us
or not. We are frozen by your indecision.

FEBRUARY 14TH

Red Roses bloom on this
Gray day.

Boundless love melts
Ice-laced snow and

Expansive romance heats up
A frozen February.

Suddenly hearty hearts calm
Wild winds

As a clever Cupid
Seduces Seasons, warms Winters.

BETWEEN THE SEASONS

Does anyone really care about the
gray days that fall between
the Winter and the
Spring?

Those hours, abandoned and
ignored, are tossed about
by careless, endless
winds.

And all the while we may slip
in and out of love, our
hearts and hurts
unnoticed

Since the Seasons seem neglected
as do our passions, when moody mornings
ignore the promise of playful
nights.

NARCISSISM

Some people only say:
"I
Me
I…Me…I"

too afraid to ask about
you or us

only able to talk with
"I" or "Me"

because talking about

you or us
takes away from
"I" or "Me"
and leaves them

scared, alone and only

i.

VALENTINE'S WHISPERS

How quiet romance can be.
One need speak in whispers
If even that.

Silence becomes the speech
Of tenderness
As deafness shouts in language
Only passion hears.

And to be heard all
Two need do is listen to the
Soft sweet sounds called love.

FOUL
(Psychotherapy 1)

He didn't talk
for six months when
we sat in my office and
I mused out loud about his silence
and what he must be thinking.

And I gave him medication
which made his body as motionless
as his words.

Until the day I
saw him in the gym and
we played some one-on-one.

When I blocked his jump-shot
from the top of the key, he
stopped and said, "You fouled me."
And then we talked.

FLIGHT
(Psychotherapy 2)

Once,
she
told me,
that she feels
Like a pigeon in a cage
on top of a brownstone
in a black and white documentary.

And
I come
to let her
out of her cage
twice a week

To move
about the world
in gentle rage and hope

No longer trapped
within herself.

So she can
feel
against the wind
and fly.

PERSONA
(Psychotherapy 3)

Analytic mask
I
hate
the analytic mask.

Because
if you scratch it
and peek beneath
I am just an old happy
sad basketball player

who likes
to laugh in the deli
and tell jokes in the Summer
at the pool in the park

and hold
people who love me.

Sometimes
I can't breathe
under the analytic mask.

APPOINTMENTS
(Psychotherapy 4)

That experience when
two people
share a common link
for a piece of time.

Where each one
sees me differently
although I am consistent
soft, strong

But not guarded
or cold, just trying
to give some room
without judgment.

And we sit together
with our wandering words
hoping to
cut the past goodbye

As an escape
into freedom and
a future filled
with wonder and will.

ACTION/CAMERA

Up against
the painted set of
obese office buildings
and short slim discount stores

we push past
each other like
over-acting extras in a
big budget Hollywood movie

and cued by
urban excessive special effects
we speak our happy angry
hopeful lines

until
the City cuts
and prints another
full featured day.

CYCLES

The March moon
always beats me home.

With a distant
full faced smirk

it teases me
from far, far away

playing hide and seek
behind busy urban evenings.

Alas, I always lose
no matter how fast I run.

Maybe
next month

Or perhaps
the month after.

SPRING

Who could have imagined
that the buds buried deep
beneath the ceaseless snow
might survive the
cold cruel months
called Winter?

That Season knew no kindness
while sleet slighted lovers
and storms broke hearts.
But now at last flowers flourish
as Spring springs forth in
full bloomed blossoms.

NEW YORK SUMMER INTERLUDE

It is oppressive
hot
August

on Columbus Avenue and 86th Street
as the red light
stops me next to her.

She seems
ageless
frail
stately
in a shetland sweater
and discarded designer coat.

In our unavoidable
momentary
Manhattan eye contact
I witness generations of New York
upon her creased handsome face.

And clutched in her hand
is a neat overstuffed
Saks shopping bag
which holds the symbols of her past
and the means
to her future.

SUMMER MOMENTS

The wide and deep
and muggy morning
moves in silent entropy.

Passive pieces of time
are emptied of energy
depleted of work.

Only the trees seem to labor
to stand erect, leaves weighted
with last night's lingering dew.

Too hot, these Summer moments
as the day
shuffles slowly to nowhere.

JULY FOURTH AT NIGHT

Like a Summer night
newborns have no boundaries
newborns know no borders.

Mothers' milk, a hallucinogen
of newfound life induces
shapeless soothing forms —
endorphins from the soul.

Babies, rocked against a
blistered sky suggest no names for
colors; surrender fear to flesh.

Who would guess that as
these postpartum months unfold
days would have structure
that dusk might bring a holiday.

Intoxicated by nurturance, early
evening induces endless daydreams.
Inside and outside probably

Bear little distinction and
stars and stripes hold no loyalty.
Only the warmth of a mother's breast
cools the hearty heat.

And as neonates ignore celebrations
only separation or abandonment
stirs their unjudged spirits.

In the end, connections, not
fireworks spark their tiny hearts.
Damning autonomy, infants won't be
weaned, July Fourth or not.

THANKSGIVING PARADES

As we wander through the decades
on these festive Wednesday nights
our family ritual never changes
when we rendezvous again with
old friends near Central Park.

At first we spot them, flat, lifeless
and empty. Then slowly each one
swells up to greet us: Snoopy yawns
and stretches while his crooked smile
fills his face.

And Popeye, tethered in the Autumn
air appears broad and buoyant while
Garfield billows fat and playful
after his catnipped helium feast.
And my daughters who used to ride

My shoulders now lean against
their sturdy boyfriends as this holiday
becomes more full, more textured
along with the generations
of Thanksgiving Eves.

NEW YEAR

Standing in a
snowfall of dried out pine needles
and last week's Christmas paper

I hold you
holding me

and watching the
old year drift away on
December's fading TV screen

we kiss the month
goodnight and

hug the
promise of each other
and this bright bold new year.

LOVE'S LEASE

When she isn't looking
I look at her
and see that
she owns my Love
and I lease from her.

And when she isn't watching
I watch her
and know that
she bought my Soul
and I rent from her.

I am the lucky tenant
who lives in Joy
with a "No Vacancy" sign
above the Apartment of
my Heart.